Wacky WORD GAMES

MARGIE GOLICK

Illustrated by
JANE CHURCHILL

Pembroke Publishers Limited

Contents

For Suzannah and Lena
And for Kathy and Karyn

© 1995 Margie Golick, text
© 1995 Jane Churchill, illustrations

Pembroke Publishers Limited
538 Hood Road
Markham, Ontario L3R 3K9, Canada

Canadian Cataloguing in Publication Data

Golick, Margaret
    Wacky word games

ISBN 1-55138-029-3

1. Word games - Juvenile literature. 2. Puzzles - Juvenile literature. I. Churchill, Jane II. Title.

GV1507.W8G8 1995   j793.73   C95-931395-8

Printed and bound in Canada
9 8 7 6 5 4 3 2 1

Some WORDS About Word GAMES

You can play word games by yourself, with a friend, or with a group. Because you don't need any special equipment, you can play word games anytime, anywhere — sitting around at home, walking to school, washing the dishes, riding in the car — even on a desert island!

Some of the games in **Wacky Word Games** have picture clues as well as word clues. Look carefully! Don't worry if an answer doesn't come to you right away. It's okay to puzzle awhile about a puzzle — and really satisfying when the solution finally pops into your head.

Turn the page, pick up a pencil and paper, and put your brain to work. As you tangle with these terrific brain teasers, you'll discover a whole new world of word fun!

Quick! How many words can you think of that rhyme with **thin**? What new words can you make using only the letters in **telephone**? Can you figure out how to turn **lead** into **gold**?

Wacky Word Games is filled with brain-boggling word games. Sound-alike words, rhyming words, different words created from the same letters, words that sound alike but are spelled differently — they're all here and many more.

Fickle Pickle

What rhymes with **spy**?
Eye, pie, necktie …
Each word on the list has several picture rhymes: there are more than 40 possible answers. See how many you can spy!

spy • THIN • *fickle*
sing • wee • **soon**
KNOCK • HOOT

5

Rhyme Time

What's a large hog?
A big pig.
A plump kitten?
A fat cat.

Find more rhyming word pairs with the same meaning as the words in the clues.

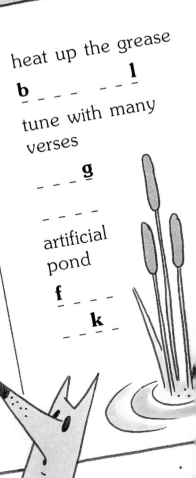

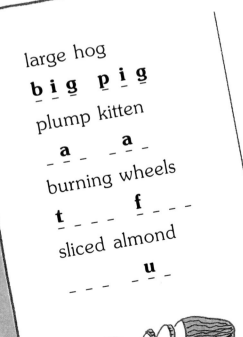

large hog
b i g   p i g

plump kitten
_ **a** _   _ **a** _

burning wheels
t _ _ _   **f** _ _ _

sliced almond
_ _ **u** _
_ _ _ _

heat up the grease
b _ _ _   _ _ **l**

tune with many verses
_ _ _ **g**
_ _ _ _

artificial pond
f _ _ _
_ **k**

spray water over the garbage

s p l _ _ _ _

_ _ _ _ **s h**

slightly wet postage

_ _ _ _

s t _ _ _ _

fight over baby's toy

_ _ _ _ _ **l e**

_ _ _ _ _ **l e**

van with its wheels in the mud

_ _ _ _ _

t r _ _ _ _

too much thinking

b r _ _ _ _

s t r _ _ _ _

introduced to the animal doctor

_ _ _ _ _ _ **t**

final explosion

_ _ **s t** _

_ _ _ _ _

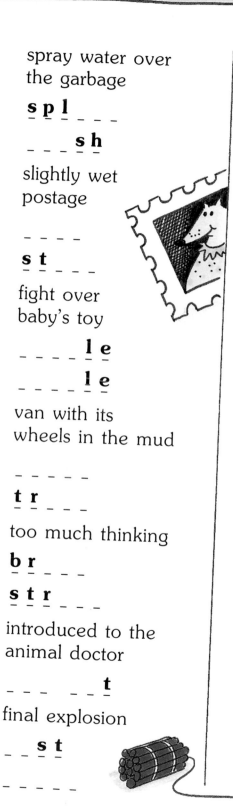

cunning insect

_ **l** _ _ **l** _

distant light in the sky

_ **a r** _ _

_ _ _ _

plane ride after dark

_ _ **g h** _

_ _ _ _ _ _

gate where you pay an entrance fee

t _ _ _ _

w _ _ _ _ _

baseball player who gained weight

_ _ _ _ **e r**

_ _ **t t** _ _

boxer who lost weight

_ _ **g h** _ _

_ _ _ _ **t e r**

cruel and selfish monarch

_ _ _ _

_ _ _ **e e** _

rattler's pains

s _ _ _ _ _ , _

_ **c h** _ _

William's medicine

_ _ _ _ , **s**

_ _ _ _

burnt breakfast treat

a w _ _ _

_ **f f** _ _

cause of seasickness

o _ _ _ _ _

_ _ **t i o n**

finished writing a short letter

_ _ **o** _ _

_ _ _ _

7

Rhyme Time II

There are more than 30 pairs of rhyming words in these pictures. Can you find the **spare chair**, the **mouse house**, the **same name**? Terrific! Now put your eagle-eyes to work to find the rest.

9

Collection

Detection

Hector is a collector. He collects all sorts of things and puts them in containers with rhyming names. For example, he has collected **jars of stars**.

Look at the pictures and figure out what else Hector has collected.

11

more Collection Detections

If you were like Hector, what would you keep in each collection?

HECTOR'S

crates of **eights**

racks of

bins of

piles of

bales of

rooms of

pockets of

bunches of

scoops of

beds of

nests of

tubs of

crocks of

plates of

cages of

jugs of

tables of

racks of

vans of

rows of

lines of

batches of

carts of

mounds of

pairs of

totes of

hills of

wads of

shelves of

traxs of

cribs of

drums of

lakes of

oceans of

caves of

sacks of

A little Alliteration

You use alliteration when you include words in sentences or phrases that start with the same sound. Newspaper and magazine headlines often use alliteration to grab our attention.

Make up your own "headlines" for these pictures. Here are some ideas to get you started: **Creepy Creature Crossly Crunches Crisp Carrot,** or **Massive Monster Moodily Munches Morsel of Meatless Meal.**

Now that you've warmed up, try creating a story to go with your headings, using as much alliteration as you can.

PLAYOFF SCORES

The Nose KNOWS

When two or more words sound the same but have different meanings, they are called "homophones." Sniff out a homophone, or sound-alike word, for each of these words.

At least five of the words on the list have additional homophones. What are they? Can you think of other homophone word pairs?

son
hair
wring
tails
brake
prints
tow
genes

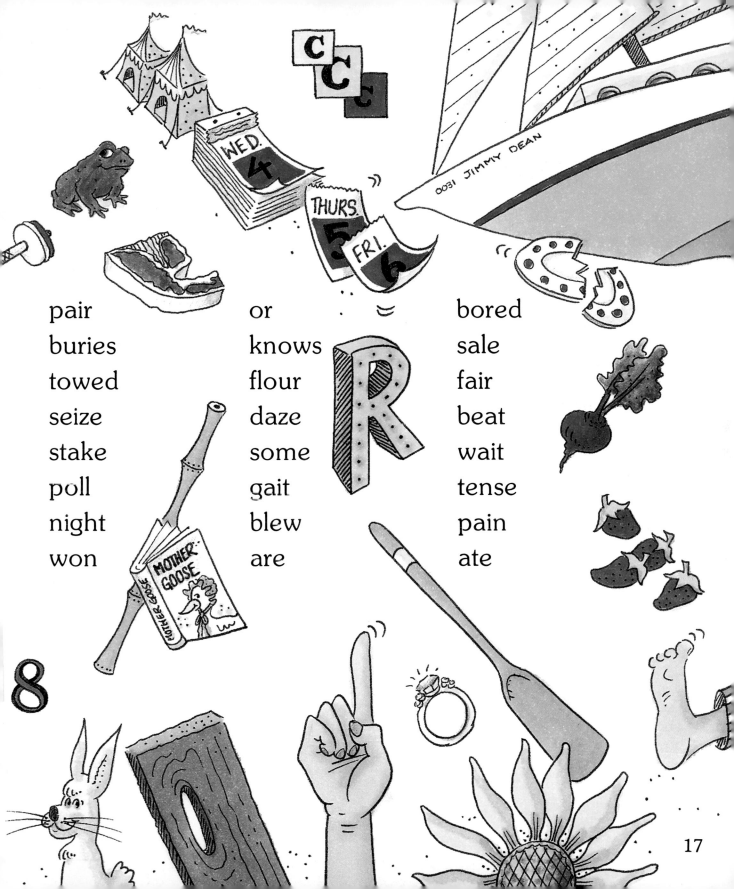

pair	or	bored
buries	knows	sale
towed	flour	fair
seize	daze	beat
stake	some	wait
poll	gait	tense
night	blew	pain
won	are	ate

8

Write

Right

What's a teddy with no clothes?
A **bare bear**.
A quick hunger strike?
A **fast fast**.
Use the word clues to find more sound-alike word pairs (homophones). The words can have the same spelling or a different spelling, but they must sound the same.

teddy with
no clothes
b a r e
b e a r

print
properly
w _ _ _ _
r _ _ _ _

quick
hunger
strike
f _ _ _ _
f _ _ _ _

listened to
the cows
_ **e a** _ _ _
_ _ _ _ _

looks at
the oceans
_ _ **e** _
_ _ **a** _

conceal
an animal
pelt
_ _ _ _
_ _ _ _

cool off
someone who
loves sports
_ _ _
_ _ _

18

early
spring
hike

M _ _ _ _ _

_ _ _ _ _

---

aircraft that's
not fancy

p _ _ **i** _

_ _ **a** _ _

---

highest
spinner
in the pile

_ _ _ _

_ _ **p**

---

flower growing
in a factory

_ _ _ _ _

_ _ _ _ _

---

gave lessons
to a small
child

_ **a u** _ _ _

t o t

---

spun
the
globe

_ _ _ _ _ _ **e d**

w _ _ _ _ _

---

was
lonesome
for the fog

_ _ **s s** _ _

_ _ _ _ _

---

lamp
that's not
heavy

_ _ _ _ _ _

_ _ _ _ _

---

finished eating
more than seven

_ _ _

_ _ _ _

---

lost two out of three

w _ _ _ _ _

---

noticed the carpenter's tool

_ _ _ _ _ _

---

choose the tool
to go with
a shovel

_ _ _ _

_ _ _ _

---

jokes
with the
children

_ _ _ **s** _

_ _ _ _ **s**

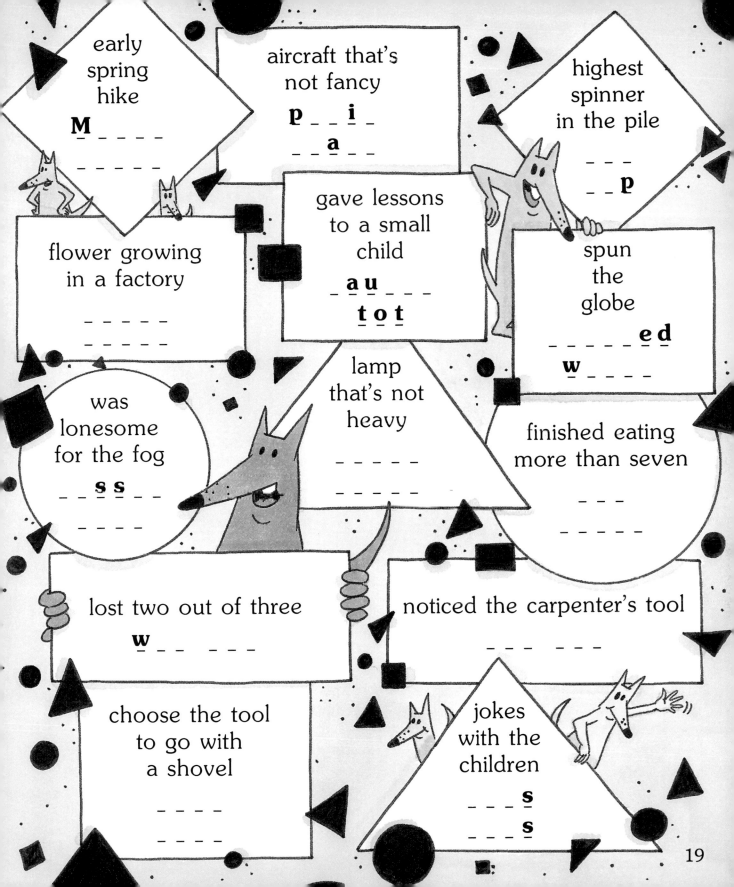

19

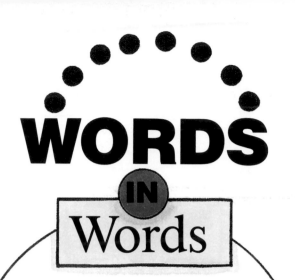

WORDS IN Words

What's in spaghetti?
No — not tomatoes and noodles.
Try **ship, tea, eight** and **pages**.
  Here's a list of all the new words found by using only the letters in spaghetti. The record number is 70. Can you find more?

example:

spaghetti

2-letter words

as	he
is	it

3-letter words

set	tag	pig	tea
pet	sag	gap	pea
get	hag	sap	sea
sat	has	sit	the
pat	gas	pit	tip
hat	his	hit	hip
tat	tap	peg	sip

4-letter words

this	hate	stag
that	page	shag
ship	sage	sigh
past	gist	site
pest	gash	tape
test	gasp	gape
pate	spit	step
gate	spat	peas

5-letter words

sight	tithe
tight	shape
paste	phase
taste	state
spate	pages
eight	spite

6-letter words

height

Can you break the record?

Make new words from each of the words listed here. Use only the letters in the word. The number after each word tells you the record number of new words found so far. Can you break the record?

meatballs (49)
hospitals (65)
danger (22)
concentration (71)
hexagon (19)
telephone (38)
refrigerator (55)
automobile (70)

Can you guess?

Which of these words makes more new words —
reading or **arithmetic**?

Which of these words makes the most new words — **September, November** or **February**?

Which day of the week makes the most new words?

How many new words can you make from your first name? Your last name? Your friends' names?

Scrambled

Words

Hte tteerls ni heset rodws era ldescamrb! (The letters in these words are scrambled.) Sort them out to find the real words.

Start by unscrambling the titles to find out the kinds of words contained in each list. For clues, look at the pictures — all the unscrambled words are there.

How many words did you unscramble? All of them? That's **tareg**!

minalas

drib	**lutter**
shif	**fragife**
kasen	**tenahelp**
riget	**yonkem**
leas	**balm**
noil	**batrib**

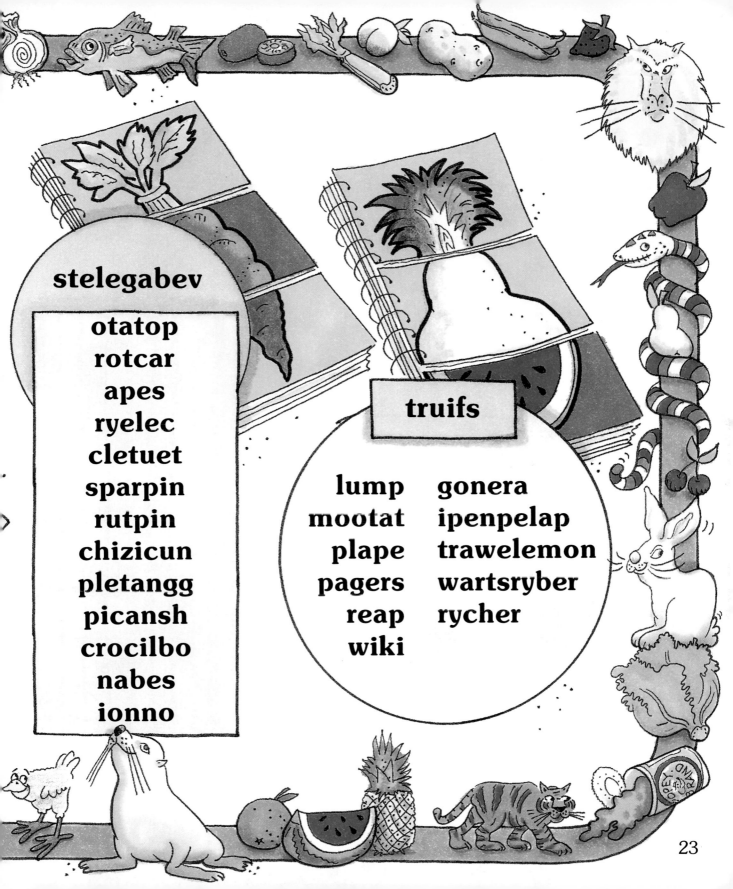

stelegabev

- otatop
- rotcar
- apes
- ryelec
- cletuet
- sparpin
- rutpin
- chizicun
- pletangg
- picansh
- crocilbo
- nabes
- ionno

truifs

lump	gonera
mootat	ipenpelap
plape	trawelemon
pagers	wartsryber
reap	rycher
wiki	

SPIT OUT THE PITS

The letters in **spit** can be moved around to spell **pits**. When two or more words have exactly the same letters in a different order, they are called anagrams.

Can you match up each anagram with its picture?

lemon
shrub
tries
calm
stake
mile
palm
petal

pests
stew
dairy
wolves
beard
stack
rats
spill

grin
spare
could
slip
stun
ocean
stop
was

flow
sale
art
hose
cheap
iced
plate
eat

Fill in the blanks with anagrams.

Eating cherries won't give you fits
if you're always careful to _ _ _ _
out the _ _ _ _.

If I **c o u l d** fly
I'd be so proud,
I'd fly my plane
Right through
a _ _ _ _ _.

Professor Paul was heard to mutter
About the slipperiness of butter.
Whenever he tried to butter his _ _ _ _ _
He buttered his long white _ _ _ _ _ instead.

Can you find more than one anagram?

Some words have more than one anagram. For example, the letters in **eat** can be moved around to spell **tea** and **ate**.

Find as many anagrams as you can for these words.

mate • vile • slime stop • steal

Read

Dear

Here's your chance to create some anagrams (words spelled with the same letters, but the letters are in a different order).

Use the word clues to find anagram pairs.

divide up
the rabbits
s h a r e
h _ _ _ _

study
your book,
darling
r e a d

_ _ _ _

creature that
comes around
after dark
n _ _ _ _
t h _ _ _

large cup for
holding something
you chew

_ _ _
m _ _

adds water
to meat
and vegetable
dish
_ _ **t s**
_ _ **e w**

revise
reducing
plan
e _ _ **t**

_ _ _ _

misplace
bottom part
of shoe

_ _ _ _
s _ _ _

26

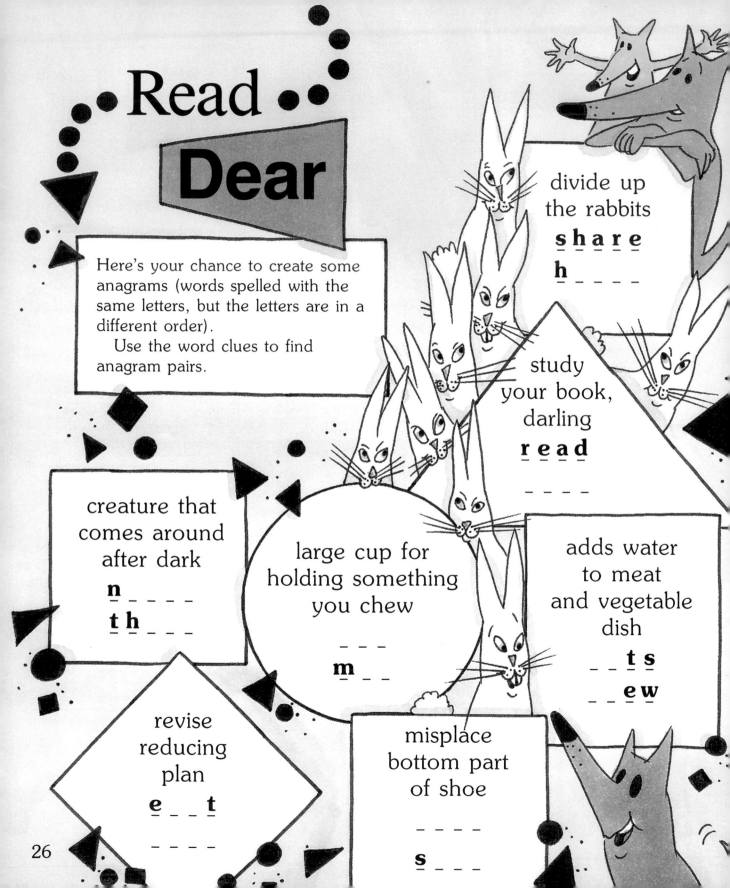

wide
wooden
plank

_ _ _ _ _

_ _ _ _ _

center of
our planet

<u>e</u> _ _ _ _

_ _ _ _ _

turn
to look at
a small
restaurant

_ _ _ _

_ **f** _ _

an
inexpensive
fruit

_ _ _ _ _

_ _ _ **c** _

keeps
jars for
flowers

<u>**s**</u> _ _ _ _

<u>**v**</u> _ _ _

had
the feeling
that everyone
had gone,
leaving me
behind

<u>**f**</u> _ _ _

<u>**l**</u> _ _ _

track down
wooden box

<u>**t r**</u> _ _ _

c r _ _ _

puts
certain
insects
in order

<u>**f**</u> _ _ _ _

<u>**f**</u> _ _ _ _

twirl
something
you try to hit
when
bowling

<u>**s p**</u> _ _

p _ _ _ **s**

very
fancy
store

p _ _ _

_ _ _ **p**

keeps
graph of
potato and pasta
eaten

c <u>h</u> _ _ _ _

_ _ _ _ **c <u>h</u>**

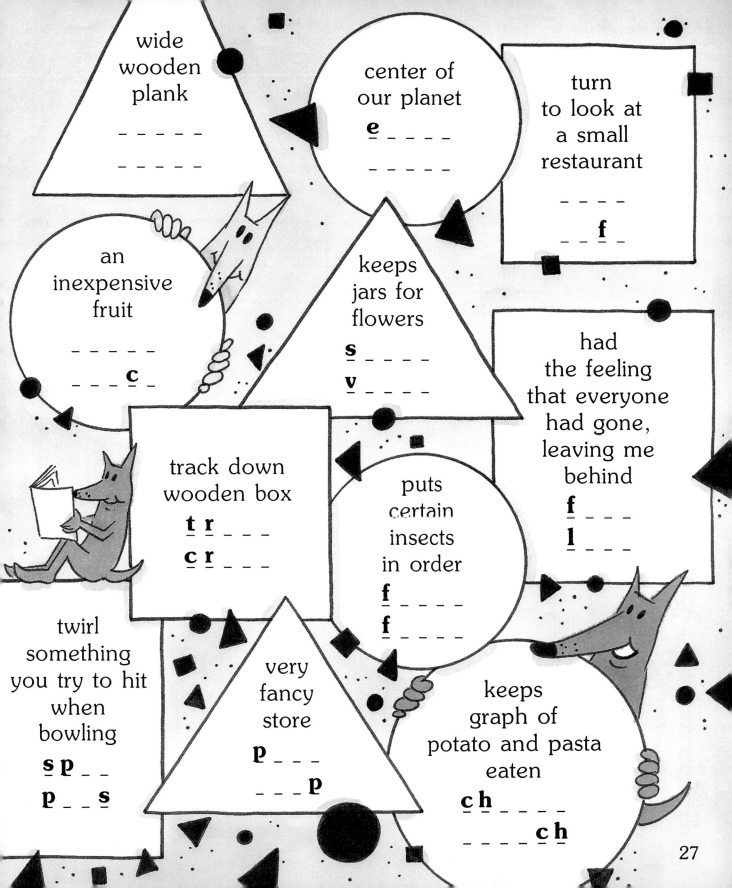

27

Turning Lead into Gold

Have you ever dreamed of being a magician? Now you can turn **lead** into **gold** — by changing one letter at a time.

The challenge is to make the change in a certain number of moves. Each move must produce a real word.

In every case there may be several ways of doing it. Here are two ways you can change **sun** to **hot** in four moves.

| cat |
| - - - |
| d o g |
| - - - |
| r a t |

l e a d
h _ _ _
_ _ _ _
_ **o** _
g o l d

| Mom |
| - - - |
| - - - |
| - - - |
| D a d |

s u n	s u n
n u n	**b** u n
n u **t**	b u **t**
h u **t**	**h** u **t**
h **o** t	h **o** t

| h i m |
| - - - |
| h e r |

| s i x |
| - - - |
| - - - |
| t e n |

| h u g |
| - - - |
| h i t |

| h a t |
| - - - |
| c a p |

| p i t c h |
| - - - - - |
| c a t c h |

28

east
- - - -
- - - -
west

sick
- - - -
- - - -
- - - -
well

ship
- - - -
- - - -
- - - -
- - - -
boat

feet
- - - -
- - - -
head

car
- - -
- - -
- - -
bus

cup
- - -
- - -
mug

hand
- - - -
- - - -
- - - -
foot
- - - -
- - - -
shoe
- - - -
boot

warm
- - - -
- - - -
- - - -
cold

mat
- - -
- - -
rug

box
- - -
bag

Peculiar Preferences

Read this poem and use the clues to figure out why Jilly has such peculiar preferences.

**Jilly Williams is pretty funny.
She likes weather cool and sunny;
Spring and winter make her mad.
Fall and summer make her glad.
She likes coffee, never tea.
She hates a bush, but likes a tree.
She eats beef, but won't touch ham.
She likes jelly, she shuns jam.
She rides scooters, can't stand bikes.
What else do you think Jilly likes?**

Clue: Make a list of the things Jilly likes, and look carefully at the words. What do they have in common?

When you figure out the reason why Jilly likes certain things and not others, look at the pictures to find all the other things she would like.

Bob Bix is just a wee bit odd.
He'll eat a pea that's in a pod.
Won't eat a beet or chew a carrot.
He has a pet. It's not a parrot.
He has a dog. He has a cat.
He hates his ball, but loves his bat.
He likes the number two, but then
he's also fond of six and ten.
He wears a cap, not scarf or gloves.
Can you tell what else Bob Bix loves?

Clue: Make a list of Bob's likes.
It's as easy as 1-2-3.

Look at the pictures and find other things
Bob would like.

Play "**Peculiar Preferences**" with
friends. Take turns thinking up likes
or dislikes to go with names. The
other players figure out the rule.
For example:

**Margie Golick likes making glue,
minding gerbils, mashing garbage,
munching gingersnaps and meeting
gorillas.** Which does she prefer:
mowing grass or picking flowers?

**Jane Churchill flies a plane but not
a helicopter, rides a train but not a
bus, walks down a lane but not a
road.** Would she like to live in Portugal
or Spain?

BE PREPARED

Hints and Answers

Part of the fun of word games is that there are many "right" answers. Here are some of the answers; yours might be different. You may even find answers we didn't think of.

Fickle Pickle (pages 4-5) — **spy**: pie, eye, butterfly, die, necktie, sky, "Y"; **thin**: pin, fish fin, tin, twin, skin, chin, grin; **fickle**: pickle, nickel, sickle; **sing:** king, sling, string, ring, wing, sting; **wee**: tea, bee, "3", tree, pea, "V", "T", knee; **soon**: loon, balloon, spoon, moon, June, raccoon; **knock:** wok, rock, clock, sock; lock, crock; **hoot**: boot, root, parachute, fruit.

Rhyme Time (pages 6-7) — tire fire; cut nut; boil oil; long song; fake lake; splash trash; damp stamp; rattle battle; stuck truck; brain strain; met vet; last blast; sly fly; far star; night flight; ticket wicket; fatter batter; lighter fighter; mean queen; snake's aches, Bill's pills; awful waffle; ocean motion; wrote note.

Rhyme Time II (pages 8-9) — red bed; sick chick; rug bug; blue shoe; toe bow; mouse house; flat mat; green bean; floor door; cellar dweller; middle fiddle; square pair; mole hole; pup cup; hare tear; broom room; hall wall; same name; sad lad; Bob's jobs; bug hug; fat rat; hen's pens; nice slice; pink drink; sweet treat; big wig; make cake; cookbook; chowder powder; fix mix; spare chair; bat hat; small ball; block's socks; snail trail.

Collection Detection (pages 10-11) — cans of fans; mugs of bugs; spoons of moons; hats of rats; boot of loot; dish of fish; books of crooks; strings of rings; trunk of junk; cups of pups; cubes of tubes; bags of rags; cases of aces; pots of dots; caps of maps; pails of snails; bowls of rolls; urns of ferns.

A Little Alliteration (pages 14-15) — No two people will say the same thing here. Did you notice who was watching Billy bouncing on the bed? Who played ping-pong for a parrot on a perch?

The Nose Knows (pages 16-17) — son-sun; hair-hare; wring-ring; tails-tales; brake-break; prints-prince; tow-toe; genes-jeans; pair-pear; buries-berries; towed-toad; seize-Cs; stake-steak; poll-pole; night-knight; won-one; or-oar; knows-nose; flour-flower; daze-days; some-sum; gait-gate; blew-blue; are-R; bored-board; sale-sail; fair-fare; beat-beet; wait-weight; tense-tents; pain-pane; ate-eight.

Write Right (pages 18-19) — heard herd; sees seas; fast fast; hide hide; write right; fan fan; March march; plant plant; missed mist; won one; pick pick; plain plane; taught tot; light light; top top; whirled world; ate eight; saw saw; kids kids.

Scrambled Words (pages 22-23) — **Animals:** bird, fish, snake, tiger, seal, lion, turtle, giraffe, elephant, monkey, lamb, rabbit. **Vegetables:** potato, carrot, peas, celery, lettuce, parsnip, turnip, zucchini, eggplant, spinach, broccoli, beans, onion. **Fruits:** plum, tomato, apple, grapes, pear, kiwi, orange, pineapple, watermelon, strawberry, cherry.

Spit Out the Pits (pages 24-25) — melon; brush; tires; clam; steak; lime; lamp; plate; steps; west; diary; vowels; bread; tacks; star; pills; ring; pears; cloud; lips; nuts; canoe; pots; saw; wolf; seal; rat; shoe; peach; dice; petal; tea. spit/pits; could/cloud; bread/beard.

Read, Dear (pages 26-27) — night thing; edit diet; gum mug; lose sole; wets stew; broad board; cheap peach; trace crate; spin pins; posh shop; earth heart; saves vases; files flies; face café; felt left; charts starch.

Peculiar Preferences (pages 30-31) — Jilly loves berries, puzzles, zippers and at least 57 other things. Bob likes the map, the sun, the pig and at least 22 other things. Did you find them all?